Team Spirit

THE ATLANTA BRAVES

BY

MARK STEWART

Content Consultant
James L. Gates, Jr.
Library Director
National Baseball Hall of Fame and Museum

NORWOOD HOUSE PRESS

CHICAGO, ILLINOIS

Norwood House Press
P.O. Box 316598
Chicago, Illinois 60631

For information regarding Norwood House Press, please visit our website at:
www.norwoodhousepress.com or call 866-565-2900.

All photos courtesy AP/Wide World Photos, Inc. except the following:
Black Book Archives—Goodwin & Co. (7 top); Piedmont Corporation (7 bottom);
Dell Publishing (18 inset); Old Judge & Gypsy Queen (34 left); Editions Rencontre (35 bottom);
Gum, Inc. (36); Exhibit Supply Co. (40 top); Sports Stars Publishing (40 bottom);
John Klein (15 & 38); Topps Inc. (21, 22, 35 top & 41); Author's Collection (6, 9 & 34 top);
Bowman Gum Co. (43); Jed Jacobsohn/Getty Images (cover image).
Special thanks to Topps, Inc.

Editor: Mike Kennedy
Designer: Ron Jaffe
Consulting Editor: Steve Krasner
Project Management: Black Book Partners, LLC.

Special thanks to: Kathleen Baxter, Amanda Jones, Tara Lockwood, Laura Peabody, and Nancy Volkman.

LIBRARY OF CONGRESS CATALOGING-IN-PUBLICATION DATA

Stewart, Mark, 1960-
  The Atlanta Braves / by Mark Stewart ; content consultant James L. Gates, Jr.
    p. cm. -- (Team spirit)
  Includes bibliographical references and index.
  ISBN-13: 978-1-59953-000-0 (library ed. : alk. paper)
  ISBN-10: 1-59953-000-7 (library ed. : alk. paper) 1. Atlanta Braves (Baseball
team)--Juvenile literature. I. Title. II. Series.

GV875.A8S83 2006
796.357'64'09758231--dc22

                                                          2005026476

COVER PHOTO: The Atlanta Braves celebrate after winning
the league championship in 1999.

Table of Contents

SPORTS WORDS & VOCABULARY WORDS: In this book, you will find many words that are new to you. You may also see familiar words used in new ways. The glossary on page 46 gives the meanings of baseball words, as well as "everyday" words that have special baseball meanings. These words appear in **bold type** throughout the book. The glossary on page 47 gives the meanings of vocabulary words that are not related to baseball. They appear in ***bold italic type*** throughout the book.

Meet the Braves

To most baseball teams, winning is a goal. For the Atlanta Braves, winning is an art. You see, it takes more than skill to reach first place and stay there. It takes a love of the game.

The Braves love to play baseball, and fans in Atlanta love the Braves. No matter how close the score, they believe their team will find a way to win. Sometimes the Braves win with good pitching, sometimes with good hitting. Usually, it is a little of each.

The Braves are smart runners and excellent fielders. They learn these skills and *techniques* in the **minor leagues**, so they are ready when they get to the **major leagues**. Every player on the Braves knows his job, and every player is prepared to do his job. When someone is having a bad game, or is injured, another player can go into the game and take his place. If you are an Atlanta Brave, this is what winning is all about.

This book tells the story of the Braves, which began more than 100 years ago. They have played in other cities. They have had different names. One thing, however, has never changed. The team has always made baseball fun!

The starters get high fives from the substitutes after another Braves victory.

Way Back When

The Braves have been playing in Atlanta since 1966. Before that, they played in Milwaukee, Wisconsin. Before that, they played in Boston, Massachusetts. The story of the Braves actually begins in the 1870s, when they were called the Red Stockings. They had the best team in the United States. In 1876, Boston was one of eight teams that formed the **National League (N.L.)**. They changed their name to Red Caps that season.

The Red Caps had many of the best players in baseball, including Deacon White, Jim O'Rourke, and Tommy Bond. The team's manager was Harry Wright. His brother, George, played shortstop for the Red Caps.

The Red Caps became the Boston Beaneaters in the 1880s. A new group of stars led this team. These players included

HARRY WRIGHT

Harry Wright, a player and manager on the team in the 1870s. During this time, the Boston club was the best in all of baseball.

TOP: "King" Kelly, the team's most popular player in the 1800s.
BOTTOM: Al Mattern in the uniform of the "Rustlers."

Hugh Duffy, Tommy McCarthy, Bobby Lowe, Mike "King" Kelly, John Clarkson, and Kid Nichols. Each is now in the **Hall of Fame**. In all, Boston won the N.L. **pennant** eight times during the 1800s.

By the early 1900s, the team's stars had all retired. This time there were no good young players to replace them. Boston went many years without a *competitive* club. The team changed its name from Beaneaters, to Nationals, to Doves, to Rustlers—but nothing helped.

In 1912, the team became the Braves. Two years later, the Braves found themselves in last place in the middle of July. Then something wonderful happened. The team got "hot," everyone played to the best of their abilities, and the Braves ended up winning the **World Series**.

The Braves went 34 years before they reached the World Series again. In 1948, they played the Cleveland Indians but lost, four games to two.

The Braves shared Boston with another team, the Red Sox. Unfortunately, there were not enough baseball fans in Boston for

Milwaukee fans loved their Braves.
They showed their support by buying souvenirs like these.

two teams, so the Braves moved to Milwaukee in 1953. This was the first time a baseball team had changed cities in 50 years. The fans of Milwaukee came out to see the Braves by the millions. They had a good mix of young stars like Henry "Hank" Aaron and Eddie Mathews, and older players, like Warren Spahn and Andy Pafko. The Braves rewarded their fans by winning the pennant in 1957 and 1958.

In 1966, the Braves decided to move again. This time they went to Atlanta, Georgia. In the 1960s, there were no big-league baseball teams in the Southeast. The Braves would enjoy their greatest success in Atlanta, and find millions of new fans in this part of the country.

Henry Aaron, the best player in Braves history,
poses in a Milwaukee uniform before a 1957 game.

The Team Today

The spirit of the today's Braves can be found exactly 60' 6" away from home plate. That is the distance to the pitcher's mound. Year after year, the Braves have one of baseball's best pitching staffs. Season after season, they finish at the top of the **standings**. Five times between 1991 and 1999, they made it all the way to the World Series. The Braves won the **Eastern Division** every year from 1995 to 2005.

How do the Braves do it? The manager and pitching coach look at the players who try out for the team each spring. They choose 10 pitchers, and then fit them together like pieces in a jigsaw puzzle. Some of the players are stars, and some are not. Some are old, and some are young. If a pitcher is injured, or cannot perform his duties, then the Braves always have someone in the minor leagues who can take his place. When you hear about the "pitching *tradition*" of the team, this is what it means.

The Atlanta players jump for joy after winning the
National League pennant in 1996.

Home Turf

The Braves play in Turner Field, which is located a few minutes from downtown Atlanta. Turner Field was built recently, but it has the spirit of an old-time ballpark. It was finished in time for for the **Summer Olympics** of 1996, and the Braves moved in at the start of the 1997 season.

Turner Field was built next to Fulton County Stadium, the Braves' home from 1966 to 1996. The old park is now a parking lot, but the old bases are still marked out on the blacktop. Most people walk into Turner Field through Grand Entry Plaza. From here, you can get to popular stops such as the Braves Hall of Fame and Monument Grove. The first thing that most fans notice when they reach their seats is a Coke bottle that is 38 feet tall.

TURNER FIELD BY THE NUMBERS

- *There are 50,096 seats in Turner Field.*
- *The distance from home plate to the left field foul pole is 335 feet.*
- *The distance from home plate to the right field foul pole is 330 feet.*
- *The distance from home plate to the center field fence is 401 feet.*
- *The first official Braves game in Turner Field was played on April 4, 1997.*

Turner Field is packed for the Home Run Derby in July of 2000. This annual event is held the night before each All-Star Game.

Dressed for Success

The Braves have used deep red and blue colors in their uniforms since 1946. That season, the team began wearing the famous script "Braves" design. During the 1970s, the Braves switched to bright uniforms that had a more modern look. By the end of the 1980s, the team had returned to its old uniform style.

John Smoltz models a "throwback" uniform similar to the ones the team wore in the 1970s.

From 1936 to 1940, the Braves were known as the Bees. The team colors were dark blue and gold, which made the players look a little like bees. Many fans kept calling them by their old name. They were happy when the team became the Braves again in 1940.

The baseball uniform has not changed much since the Braves began playing. It has four main parts:

- a cap or batting helmet with a sun visor;
- a top with a player's number on the back;
- pants that reach down between the ankle and the knee;
- stirrup-style socks.

The uniform top sometimes has a player's name on the back. The team's name, city, or *logo* is usually on the front. Baseball teams wear light-colored uniforms when they play at home, and darker styles when they play on the road.

For more than 100 years, baseball uniforms were made of wool *flannel* and were very baggy. This helped the sweat *evaporate* and gave players the freedom to move around. Today's uniforms are made of *synthetic* fabrics that stretch with players and keep them dry and cool.

Chipper Jones wears his uniform in the traditional style, with plenty of sock and stirrup showing.

We Won!

The fans who cheer for the Braves today have much in common with the fans who rooted for the team long ago. The team won championships in the 1870s, 1880s, and 1890s. In 1892, the Boston Beaneaters were the first ball club ever to win 100 games in a season. This team—which would one day become the Braves—won with great pitching, smart base-running, good hitting, and steady fielding.

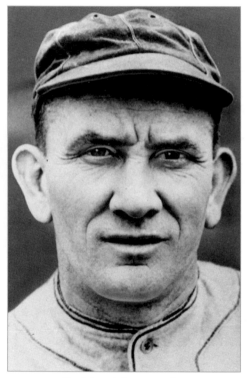

Rabbit Maranville

Once in a while, a baseball team wins a championship and no one can understand how they did it. The 1914 Braves were this kind of team. They were in last place on July 18 that season, with the mighty New York Giants far out in front. Then something magical happen. Led by their brilliant manager, George Stallings, and two scrappy infielders named Rabbit Maranville and Johnny Evers, the Braves could not lose. They not only caught the Giants—they finished more than 10 games ahead! In the 1914

Warren Spahn and Johnny Sain. They won nine games
for the Braves in the final weeks of the 1948 season.

World Series, the Braves continued their amazing play. They beat
the Philadelphia A's four games to none. This team is still called the
"Miracle Braves" almost a century later.

The Braves did not win another World Series during their time
in Boston. However, in 1948, they surprised baseball fans again by
winning another exciting pennant. The Braves found themselves in
a four-way battle for first place in the season's final month. With
pitchers Warren Spahn and Johnny Sain leading the way, they won
14 of 15 games to finish far ahead of the other teams.

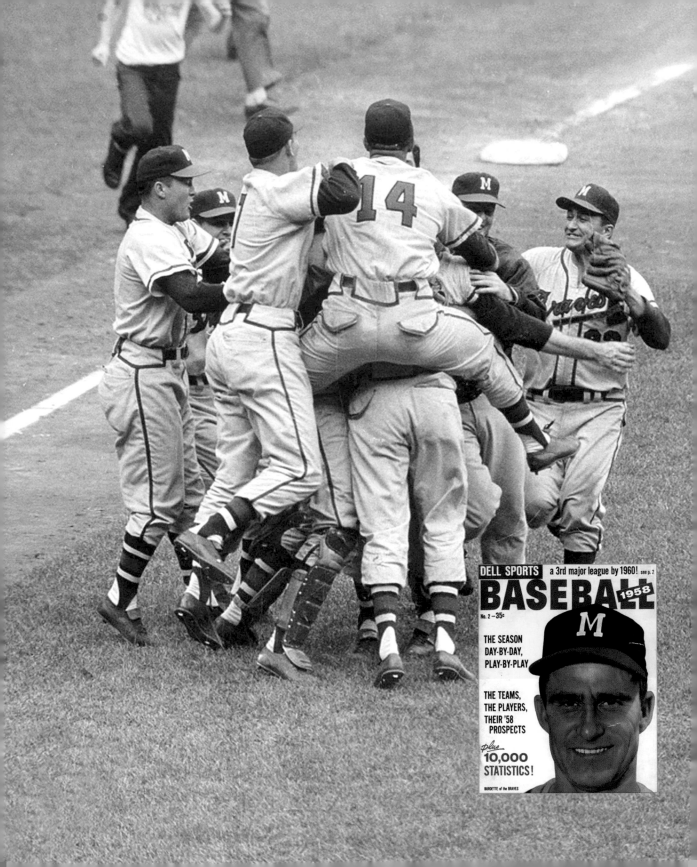

DELL SPORTS   a 3rd major league by 1960! see p. 2

BASEBALL 1958

No. 2—35¢

THE SEASON
DAY-BY-DAY,
PLAY-BY-PLAY

THE TEAMS,
THE PLAYERS,
THEIR '58
PROSPECTS

Plus
10,000
STATISTICS!

BURDETTE of the BRAVES

During their 13 years in Milwaukee, the Braves won the World Series once, in 1957. Pitcher Lew Burdette beat the New York Yankees three times and Henry Aaron hit three home runs in a thrilling series. After moving to Atlanta, the Braves waited until 1995 before they were champions again. They beat the Cleveland Indians that year, four games to two. No other team in baseball has won three championships playing in three different cities.

Since the early 1990s, the Braves have made it to the playoffs more than any other team. They have learned what it takes to win, even when they do not have the best players. In the future, other teams will look back and learn many lessons from Atlanta's amazing record.

LEFT: Pitcher Lew Burdette disappears underneath his happy teammates. He beat the New York Yankees to win the 1957 World Series.
INSET: Burdette was front-page news after giving Milwaukee its only championship. **RIGHT:** Mark Wohlers leaps into the air after pitching the Braves to the 1995 pennant. Atlanta went on to defeat the Cleveland Indians in the World Series.

Go-To Guys

To be a true star in baseball, you need more than a quick bat and a strong arm. You have to be a "go-to guy"—someone the manager wants on the pitcher's mound or in the batter's box when it matters most. Braves fans have had a lot to cheer about over the years, including these great stars...

THE PIONEERS

KING KELLY   Outfielder/Catcher

- BORN: 12/31/1857   • DIED: 11/8/1894
- PLAYED FOR TEAM: 1887 TO 1889 AND 1891 TO 1892

Mike "King" Kelly was the most popular player the team ever had while it played in Boston. He was the game's most daring runner. Whenever he was on the base paths, the fans would yell, "Slide, Kelly, slide!"

HUGH DUFFY   Outfielder

- BORN: 11/26/1866   • DIED: 10/19/1954   • PLAYED FOR TEAM: 1892 TO 1900

Hugh Duffy was the best hitter on the Boston teams of the 1890s. In 1894, he became the first batter to win the "Triple Crown" by leading the league in home runs, batting average, and **runs batted in (RBIs)**. Duffy's batting average of .438 that year is still the highest in history.

KID NICHOLS   Pitcher

- BORN: 9/14/1869   • DIED: 4/11/1953   • PLAYED FOR TEAM: 1890 TO 1901

Charlie "Kid" Nichols won 30 or more games seven times. He had a great fastball and was one of the smartest pitchers around.

WARREN SPAHN   Pitcher

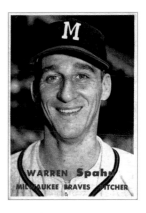

- BORN: 4/23/1921   • DIED: 11/24/2003
- PLAYED FOR TEAM: 1942 TO 1964

Warren Spahn was the Braves' best pitcher for more than 15 years. He had a good fastball and could make his pitches curve from left to right, or right to left. Spahn won 363 games—more than any left-handed pitcher in history.

EDDIE MATHEWS   Third Baseman

- BORN: 10/13/1931   • DIED: 2/18/2001   • PLAYED FOR TEAM: 1952 TO 1966

Eddie Mathews was the best fielder and hitter at his position for 10 years. He had one of the fastest swings in history. Mathews was the only man to play for the Braves in Boston, Milwaukee, and Atlanta.

HENRY AARON   Outfielder

- BORN: 2/5/1934   • PLAYED FOR TEAM: 1954 TO 1974

Henry Aaron used his sharp eyes and quick wrists to smash line drives all over the field. He was chosen as an **All-Star** in 20 of his 21 years with the Braves. In 1974, Aaron became baseball's all-time home run king when he hit his 715th home run.

ABOVE: Warren Spahn   **RIGHT:** Henry Aaron

MODERN STARS

PHIL NIEKRO · Pitcher

- BORN: 4/1/1939 · PLAYED FOR TEAM: 1964 TO 1983; 1987

Phil Niekro won more than 300 games using a **knuckleball**. He could make this pitch move just as the batter was swinging, which made it almost impossible to hit. Niekro was beloved by the people of Atlanta for his loyalty to the Braves and his work for good causes in the city.

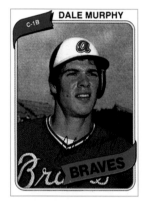

DALE MURPHY · Outfielder

- BORN: 3/12/1956 · PLAYED FOR TEAM: 1976 TO 1990

Dale Murphy was a powerful hitter, fast runner, and graceful fielder. One year he hit 30 home runs, stole 30 bases, and won the **Gold Glove** award for his excellent fielding. When Murphy retired, he had played more games in an Atlanta uniform than any other player.

TOM GLAVINE · Pitcher

- BORN: 3/25/1966 · PLAYED FOR TEAM: 1987 TO 2002

Tom Glavine was Atlanta's best left-handed pitcher during the 1990s. He had **pinpoint control** and almost never gave a batter a good pitch to hit. Glavine led the league (or tied for the lead) in wins five different times.

JOHN SMOLTZ · Pitcher

- BORN: 5/15/1967 · FIRST YEAR WITH TEAM: 1988

John Smoltz was a great "big-game" pitcher. The more pressure he felt, the better he threw. After winning more than 150 games as a **starting pitcher**, Smoltz became a **relief pitcher** for four years and had more than 150 **saves**.

GREG MADDUX   Pitcher

• BORN: 4/14/1966   • PLAYED FOR TEAM: 1993 TO 2003

Greg Maddux did some of the finest pitching ever during his 11 years with the Braves. At a time when home runs were flying out of ball parks, it was very difficult to score a run against him.

CHIPPER JONES   Third Baseman/Outfielder

• BORN: 4/24/1972   • FIRST YEAR WITH TEAM: 1993

Chipper Jones loved to bat with men on base. He had 100 or more RBIs eight years in a row. Jones won the **Most Valuable Player** award in 1999 and became one of baseball's best **switch-hitters**.

ANDRUW JONES   Outfielder

• BORN: 4/23/1977   • FIRST YEAR WITH TEAM: 1996

Andruw Jones was known for his fielding when he joined the Braves as a teenager. Soon he also was famous for his home runs. Jones hit a home run in the World Series at the age of 19. He smashed more than 300 in his first 10 years with the Braves.

LEFT: As his 1980 trading card shows, Dale Murphy began his career as a catcher and first baseman.
RIGHT: Andruw Jones launches a home run during the 2005 All-Star Game. He set a team record with 51 that season.

Legend Has It

Did Bama Rowell of the Braves inspire the writer of a famous baseball book?

LEGEND HAS IT that he did. Author Bernard Malamud was in Brooklyn's Ebbets Field on Memorial Day in 1946, for a game between the Braves and the Dodgers. Rowell hit a home run that broke a large Bulova clock. Pieces of glass rained down on outfielder Dixie Walker of the Dodgers. In Malamud's book *The Natural,* his hero, Roy Hobbs, wins the pennant with a home run that crashes into the light tower and showers the field with sparks and glass.

How did the Braves get their team name?

LEGEND HAS IT that they were named after their owner. His name was Jim Gaffney, and he was known in Boston as the "Brave of Tammany Hall." Tammany Hall was a powerful political organization. More than 80 years after Gaffney left baseball, the team is still called the Braves.

Did slugger Henry Aaron hold his bat the wrong way?

LEGEND HAS IT that he did. Aaron batted "cross-handed" when he was a teenager. He placed his right hand just above the knob of the bat, and his left hand above his right hand. Aaron was gripping the bat correctly by the time he joined the Braves, but he still had it turned the wrong way—with the label facing the catcher. This meant he was not getting the full strength of the wood behind his swing.

During the 1957 World Series, Aaron stepped to the plate and the catcher, Yogi Berra, told him that he should hold the bat so

Henry Aaron is carried off the field after his home run clinched the pennant for the Braves in 1957.

that he could read the label. "I'm not here to read," grunted Aaron. "I'm here to hit." He sure did! Aaron led all batters with 11 hits, three home runs, and a .393 batting average.

It Really Happened

In 1935, the Braves asked Babe Ruth to play for their team. He was the greatest **slugger** in history, but by this time his knees ached and he was too old to play every day. Ruth agreed to play anyway. He thought the Braves might make him the manager.

Soon it was clear that the owner, Judge Emil Fuchs, had tricked Ruth. Fuchs wanted a famous player to bring extra fans into the ball park. He would never let Ruth manage. Ruth was angry and sad. He decided it was time to retire.

Ruth agreed to go on one last road trip. In a game against the Pittsburgh Pirates, he hit a home run in the first inning, another in the third inning, and a third home run in the seventh inning. The last home run flew completely out of Pittsburgh's Forbes Field—one of the largest parks in baseball. No one had ever hit one out of Forbes Field!

That amazing home run was the last hit of Ruth's career. He was in the **lineup** a few more times so he could wave to the crowd, but before the Braves returned to Boston, Ruth told the baseball world he was leaving the game.

Babe Ruth poses between Cincinnati Reds manager Charlie Dressen and Braves manager Bill McKechnie after his first game with Boston, in 1935. Ruth hoped he would become the team's manager that year.

Team Spirit

The Atlanta Braves have fans all over the United States. Their games can be seen in millions of homes on TBS, the television network owned by Ted Turner, who also owned the Braves. Wherever the Braves play, they have fans in the stands. When the players hear their fans on the road, they feel a little closer to home.

In Atlanta, the fans in Turner Field stand up and do the "Tomahawk Chop," pretending they are Indian braves attacking the other team. They also sing a special song that echoes all over the ball park.

Former President Jimmy Carter and his wife, Rosalyn, do the Tomahawk Chop during a game in 2003. Is this an innocent fan tradition, or disrespectful to Native American heritage?

Some Native American groups do not like the name of the team, and they do not like the Tomahawk Chop. They feel that it is disrespectful to their history. The Braves used to have a **mascot** called Chief Nok-A-Homa, who danced in front of a tepee. The team agreed to stop using the mascot. In 2005, many colleges agreed to stop using Native American names for their sports teams.

Will Native American groups **persuade** professional sports teams like the Braves, Indians, Redskins, Chiefs, and Warriors to change their names some day? Will the Braves become the Bees again? This will be a very interesting **debate** to watch over the next few years.

When the Braves played the Indians in the 1995 World Series, Native American leaders spoke out against sports teams that use Native American names.

Timeline

1871
The Boston
Red Stockings
go 22–10
in their
first season.

1883
The team
changes its name
to Beaneaters.

1912
The team
changes its name
to Braves.

1936
The team
changes its
name to Bees.

1892
King Kelly leads the
team to baseball's
first 100-win season.

1914
The Braves win
the World Series.

1876
The Braves play
the first game in
National League
history.

The 1914 Boston Braves.

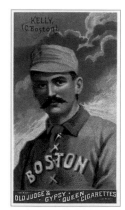

"King" Kelly

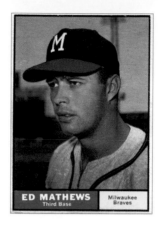

ED MATHEWS
Third Base Milwaukee Braves

LEFT: Eddie Mathews, the only person to play for the Braves in Boston, Milwaukee, and Atlanta. **RIGHT**: Javier Lopez hits a World Series home run in 1995.

1953
The Braves move to Milwaukee, Wisconsin.

1966
The Braves move to Atlanta, Georgia.

1995
The Braves win the World Series.

1940
The team changes its name back to Braves.

1957
The Braves win the World Series.

1974
Henry Aaron becomes baseball's all-time home run king.

2005
The Braves make the playoffs for the 14th year in a row.

Henry Aaron

Fun Facts

YOU GUYS ARE OLD!

The Braves are the only team to put a team on the field in every year professional baseball has been played (1871 to present).

STAR POWER

Mike "King" Kelly was the first player to sign autographs for fans. In 1891, the song "Slide, Kelly, Slide" became one of the first songs recorded for sale to the public.

Dolf Luque

BRAVE NEW WORLD

In 1914, Cuban star Dolf Luque of the Braves became the first Latino ever to pitch in the big leagues.

TOTALLY AWESOME

In 1954, first baseman Joe Adcock hit four home runs and a double in one game. His 18 total bases (4+4+4+4+2=18) is still a record.

CLEARING THE BASES

Tony Cloninger of the 1966 Braves was the first player to hit two grand slams in one game. He was not a power hitter—he was a pitcher!

Tony Cloninger

RHYME TIME

The 1948 Braves won the pennant with just two good pitchers, Warren Spahn and Johnny Sain. Fans joked that the team's plan was "Spahn and Sain...and pray for rain!"

BUY THE BOOK

The Braves were the first team to print a yearbook, in 1946. They sold 22,000 copies during the season.

WINNING PITCH

The **Cy Young Award**, which is given to the league's best pitcher each year, was won by a member of the Braves six times between 1991 and 1998.

Talking Baseball

"I don't want people to forget Babe Ruth.
I just want them to remember Henry Aaron."

— Henry Aaron, on breaking Ruth's home run record

"I love taking hits away from guys and seeing their reaction."

— Andruw Jones, on the joy of playing defense

"A pitcher must have two pitches—
one the batter is expecting, and one he isn't."

— Warren Spahn, on what it takes to win in the major leagues

Greg Maddux

"I knew right then and there that
I would fit in and be accepted."

*— Greg Maddux, remembering his first day with the Braves,
when he was invited to play golf with the other pitchers*

"Most guys, when their mom suggests something,
roll their eyes. When my mom does, I listen.
My mom knows more about baseball than
half the people in the major leagues."

— Chipper Jones, on his number-one coach

Eddie Mathews with manager Tommy Holmes in 1952.

"All I know is there's nothing like the
southern hospitality of Atlanta."
— *Tom Glavine, on his life off the field with the Braves*

"I'm just a small part of a wonderful game
that is a tremendous part of America today."
— *Eddie Mathews, who hit 493 home runs for the Braves*

For the Record

The great Braves teams and players have left their marks on the record books. These are the "best of the best"…

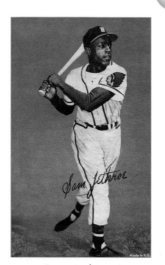

Sam Jethroe

Henry Aaron

BRAVES AWARD WINNERS

WINNER	AWARD	YEAR
Johnny Evers	Most Valuable Player	1914
Bob Elliott	Most Valuable Player	1947
Sam Jethroe	Rookie of the Year*	1950
Henry Aaron	Most Valuable Player	1957
Warren Spahn	Cy Young Award	1957
Earl Williams	Rookie of the Year	1971
Bob Horner	Rookie of the Year	1978
Dale Murphy	Most Valuable Player	1982
Dale Murphy	Most Valuable Player	1983
David Justice	Rookie of the Year	1990
Terry Pendleton	Most Valuable Player	1991
Tom Glavine	Cy Young Award	1991
Greg Maddux	Cy Young Award	1993
Greg Maddux	Cy Young Award	1994
Greg Maddux	Cy Young Award	1995
John Smoltz	Cy Young Award	1996
Tom Glavine	Cy Young Award	1998
Chipper Jones	Most Valuable Player	1999
Rafael Furcal	Rookie of the Year	2000

The Rookie of the Year award is given to the league's best first-year player.

BRAVES ACHIEVEMENTS

ACHIEVEMENT	YEAR
National Association Pennant	1872*
National Association Pennant	1873
National Association Pennant	1874
National Association Pennant	1875
N.L. Pennant Winner	1877
N.L. Pennant Winner	1878
N.L. Pennant Winner	1883
N.L. Pennant Winner	1891
N.L. Pennant Winner	1892
N.L. Pennant Winner	1893
N.L. Pennant Winner	1897
N.L. Pennant Winner	1898
N.L. Pennant Winner	1914
World Series Champions	1914
N.L. Pennant Winner	1948
N.L. Pennant Winner	1957
World Series Champions	1957
N.L. Pennant Winner	1958
N.L. Pennant Winner	1991
N.L. Pennant Winner	1992
N.L. Pennant Winner	1995
World Series Champions	1995
N.L. Pennant Winner	1996
N.L. Pennant Winner	1999

The National Association was the first professional baseball league. It lasted from 1871 to 1875.

David Justice

Greg Maddux

Pinpoints

The history of a baseball team is made up of many smaller stories. These stories take place all over the map—not just in the city a team calls "home." Match the push-pins on these maps to the Team Facts and you will begin to see the story of the Braves unfold!

TEAM FACTS

1 Boston, Massachusetts—*The team played here from 1871 to 1952.*

2 Milwaukee, Wisconsin—*The Braves played here from 1953 to 1965.*

3 Atlanta, Georgia—*The Braves have played here since 1966.*

4 Nitro, West Virginia—*Lew Burdette was born here.*

5 Mobile, Alabama—*Henry Aaron was born here.*

6 Buffalo, New York—*Warren Spahn was born here.*

7 Texarkana, Texas—*Eddie Mathews was born here.*

8 Portland, Oregon—*Dale Murphy was born here.*

9 DeLand, Florida—*Chipper Jones was born here.*

10 Detroit, Michigan—*John Smoltz was born here.*

11 Sheffield, England—*Harry Wright was born here.*

12 Willemstad, Curacao—*Andruw Jones was born here.*

Lew Burdette

Play Ball

Baseball is a game played between two teams over nine innings. Teams take one turn at bat and one turn in the field during each inning. A turn at bat ends when three outs are made. The batters on the hitting team try to reach base safely. The players on the fielding team try to prevent this from happening.

In baseball, the ball is controlled by the pitcher. The pitcher must throw the ball to the batter, who decides whether or not to swing at each pitch. If a batter swings and misses, it is a strike. If the batter lets a good pitch go by, it is also a strike. If the batter swings and the ball does not stay in fair territory (between the v-shaped lines that begin at home plate) it is called "foul," and is counted as a strike. If the pitcher throws three strikes, the batter is out. If the pitcher throws four bad pitches before that, the batter is awarded first base. This is called a base-on-balls, or "walk."

When the batter swings the bat and hits the ball, everyone springs into action. If a fielder catches a batted ball before it hits the ground, the batter is out. If a fielder scoops the ball off the ground and throws it to first base before the batter arrives, the batter is out. If the batter reaches first base safely, he is credited with a hit. A one-base hit is called a single, a two-base hit is called a double, a three-base hit is called a triple, and a four-base hit is called a home run.

Runners who reach base are only safe when they are touching one of the bases. If they are caught between the bases, the fielders can tag them with the ball and record an out.

A batter who is able to circle the bases and make it back to home plate before three outs are made is credited with a run scored. The team with the most runs after nine innings is the winner.

Anyone who has played baseball (or softball) knows that it can be a complicated game. Every player on the field has a job to do. Different players have different strengths and weaknesses. The pitchers, batters, and managers make hundreds of decisions every game. The more you play and watch baseball, the more "little things" you are likely to notice. The next time you are at a game, look for these plays:

PLAY LIST

DOUBLE PLAY—A play where the fielding team is able to make two outs on one batted ball. This usually happens when a runner is on first base, and the batter hits a ground ball to one of the infielders. The base runner is forced out at second base and the ball is then thrown to first base before the batter arrives.

HIT AND RUN—A play where the runner on first base sprints to second base while the pitcher is throwing the ball to the batter. When the second baseman or shortstop moves toward the base to wait for the catcher's throw, the batter tries to hit the ball to the place that the fielder has just left. If the batter swings and misses, the fielding team can tag the runner out.

INTENTIONAL WALK—A play when the pitcher throws four bad pitches on purpose, allowing the batter to walk to first base. This happens when the pitcher would much rather face the next batter—and is willing to risk putting a runner on base.

SACRIFICE BUNT—A play where the batter makes an out on purpose so that a teammate can move to the next base. On a bunt, the batter tries to "deaden" the pitch with the bat instead of swinging at it.

SHOESTRING CATCH—A play where an outfielder catches a short hit an inch or two above the ground, near the tops of his shoes. It is not easy to run as fast as you can and lower your glove without slowing down. It can be risky, too. If a fielder misses a shoestring catch, the ball might roll all the way to the fence.

Glossary

BASEBALL WORDS TO KNOW

ALL-STAR—A player who is selected to play in baseball's annual All-Star Game.

CY YOUNG AWARD—The trophy given to the league's best pitcher each year.

EASTERN DIVISION—A group of teams (within a league) that all play in the eastern part of the country.

GOLD GLOVE—An award given each year to baseball's best fielders.

HALL OF FAME—The museum in Cooperstown, NY where baseball's greatest players are honored. A player voted into the Hall of Fame is sometimes called a "Hall of Famer."

KNUCKLEBALL—A pitch thrown with no spin, which "wobbles" as it nears home plate. A knuckleball is held with the tips of the fingers, so the batter sees a pitcher's knuckles when he throws it.

LINEUP—The list of players who are playing in a game.

MAJOR LEAGUES—The top level of professional baseball leagues. The American League (A.L.) and National League (N.L.) make up today's major leagues. Sometimes called the "big leagues."

MINOR LEAGUES—The many professional leagues that help develop players for the major leagues.

MOST VALUABLE PLAYER (MVP)—An award given each year to the league's top player; an MVP is also selected for the World Series and All-Star Game.

NATIONAL LEAGUE (N.L.)—The older of the two major leagues; the N.L. began play in 1876 and the American League (A.L.) started in 1901.

PENNANT—A league championship. The term comes from the triangular flag awarded to each season's champion, beginning in the 1870s.

PINPOINT CONTROL—An ability to throw a pitch to a precise point.

RELIEF PITCHER—A pitcher who is brought into a game to replace another pitcher. Relief pitchers can be seen warming up in the bullpen.

RUNS BATTED IN (RBIS)—A statistic that counts the number of runners a batter drives home.

SAVES—A statistic relief pitchers earn when they get the final out of a close game.

SLUGGER—A powerful hitter.

STANDINGS—A daily list of teams, starting with the team with the best record and ending with the team with the worst record.

STARTING PITCHER—The pitcher who begins the game for his team.

SUMMER OLYMPICS—An international sports competition held every four years.

SWITCH-HITTER—A player who can hit from either side of home plate. Switch-hitters bat left-handed against right-handed pitchers, and right-handed against left-handed pitchers.

WORLD SERIES—The world championship series played between the winners of the National League and American League.

OTHER WORDS TO KNOW

COMPETITIVE—Having a strong desire to win.

DEBATE—A discussion between people who disagree on an important point.

EVAPORATE—Disappear, or turn into a vapor.

EXTRAORDINARY—Unusual, or unusually talented.

FLANNEL—A soft wool or cotton material.

LOGO—A symbol or design that represents a company or team.

MASCOT—An animal or person that brings a group good luck.

PERSUADE—To change someone's mind.

RACISTS—People who treat others unfairly because of their race.

SYNTHETIC—Made in a laboratory, not in nature.

TECHNIQUES—Specific ways of doing something.

TRADITION—A belief or custom that is handed down from generation to generation.

Places to Go
ON THE ROAD

TURNER FIELD
755 Hank Aaron Drive SE
Atlanta, Georgia 30315
(404) 577-9100

**NATIONAL BASEBALL
HALL OF FAME AND MUSEUM**
25 Main Street
Cooperstown, New York 13326
(888) 425-5633
www.baseballhalloffame.org

ON THE WEB

THE ATLANTA BRAVES   www.Bravcs.com
  • *to learn more about the Braves*

MAJOR LEAGUE BASEBALL   www.mlb.com
  • *to learn about all the major league teams*

MINOR LEAGUE BASEBALL   www.minorleaguebaseball.com
  • *to learn more about the minor leagues*

ON THE BOOKSHELVES

To learn more about the sport of baseball, look for these books at your library or bookstore:

  • January, Brendan. *A Baseball All-Star*. Chicago, IL.: Heinemann Library, 2005.

  • Kelly, James. *Baseball*. New York, NY.: DK, 2005.

  • Mintzer, Rich. *The Everything Kids' Baseball Book*. Cincinnati, OH.: Adams Media Corporation, 2004.

Index

PAGE NUMBERS IN **BOLD** REFER TO ILLUSTRATIONS.

The Team

MARK STEWART has written more than 25 books on baseball, and over 100 sports books for kids. He grew up in New York City during the 1960s rooting for the Yankees and Mets, and now takes his two daughters, Mariah and Rachel, to the same ballparks. Mark comes from a family of writers. His grandfather was Sunday Editor of *The New York Times* and his mother was Articles Editor of *Ladies Home Journal* and *McCall's*. Mark has profiled hundreds of athletes over the last 20 years. He has also written several books about his native New York and New Jersey, his home today. Mark is a graduate of Duke University, with a degree in history. He lives with his daughters and wife, Sarah, overlooking Sandy Hook, NJ.

JAMES L. GATES, JR. has served as Library Director at the National Baseball Hall of Fame since 1995. He had previously served in academic libraries for almost fifteen years. He holds degrees from Belmont Abbey College, the University of Notre Dame and Indiana University. During his career Jim has authored several academic articles and has served in an editorial capacity on multiple book, magazine and museum publications, and he also serves as host for the Annual Cooperstown Symposium on Baseball and American Culture. He is an ardent Baltimore Orioles fan and enjoys watching baseball with his wife and two children.